MW00975621

LAND OF IMPERFECTION

THE GOOD, THE BAD, THE UGLY, AND THE PRIDE

SANDY SOLOMON

978-1-945493-61-4

First published by ImPress Publishing Services 2023

Copyright © 2023 by Sandy Solomon

ISBN: 978-1-945493-61-4

LAND OF IMPERFECTION

First edition

CONTENTS

DEDICATION

In loving memory of my husband,
Paul who was my life.

PROLOGUE: THE PROMISED LAND

In *The land of imperfection,* I set forth the premise that this nation is not perfect. Of course, nothing is perfect in this life, but when America was discovered, the hope was that it would be the antidote for all the individuals fleeing other countries with harsh regimes. The early immigrants sought a new world where they would be free to worship as they pleased, free to live in perfect harmony with the land, and not be fearful of arrest and totalitarian control. The dream of America was to let people be free, to wake up each day, with the dawn making everyone's lives a fulfillment of something precious, liberty.

As Christopher Columbus and his fleet of ships set forth to discover new territories, their first landings were in Central America. They came as conquerors, pillaging the land, and enslaving the indigenous natives that lived there. Their intent was not to assure freedom and opportunity, but the domination of the people they encountered. That effort continued as they traveled from island to island in the Western Hemisphere.

Columbus never came to North America. Why do we continue to celebrate Columbus Day in the United States on the second Monday in October annually if his exploration was only in Central America?

Here we are, hundreds of years after the early explorers, Americans of the United States, trying to live the experiment of Democracy. I believe the experiment is in jeopardy. That is why I am writing this book. I love my country and believe only by examining our past can we turn things around and make America the promised land again for all people.

CHAPTER 1: THREATS

On September 9, 1776, a new country was born and named the United States Of America. Since that time, it has been far from united. When the Constitution was written, it contained an unprecedented statement: "All Men Are Created Equal." Unfortunately, we all know that was not true.

In March 1790, Congress passed the first law about who should be granted U. S. citizenship. *The Naturalization Act* allowed any free white person of "good character " who had been living in the United States for two years or longer to apply for citizenship. Without citizenship, non-white residents were denied basic constitutional protections, including the right to vote, own property, or testify in court.

Black men held in slavery in the Southern states were considered 'sub-human.'

Women were second-class citizens, controlled by their husbands, or by government rules different than those for males. Jews were discriminated against, even though a prominent Jew helped fund the Revolution. Asian immigrants were treated as unworthy to participate in this new society.

Immigrants have been coming to America from every part of the world with the belief that it was the "land of milk and honey," and that the "streets were paved with gold." They flocked to our shores dreaming of freedom and prosperity. They came here to better their lives. Many left their homelands in Europe in search of economic opportunity and religious freedom.

Did they find what they were promised?

More than 70% of all immigrants entered
the United States through Ellis Island, which
became known as the "Golden Door." It opened
in January 1892 in New York harbor, as the
U.S. First immigration station. More than 12
million immigrants would enter through the
Island between 1892 and 1954. As steamboats
sailed to Ellis Island, the Statue of Liberty greeted
the newcomers. Her inscription called out, "Give
me your tired, your poor, your huddled masses
yearning to breathe free." These famous lines
were written by a Jewish woman, Emma Lazarus.
Immigrants flocking to this country saw Lady
Liberty as a symbol of a new life, a new beginning.

When I went with my father, who had come
through Ellis Island as a six-year-old immigrant in
1913, we took the tour. The guide explained that
at the forefront of the complex, the immigrants
had to climb a long staircase to reach the second
floor. That seemed odd until you learned why. If
you were not able to climb to the second floor,

the immigrant was sent back to their original country. They were deemed unhealthy and not strong enough to be allowed into the 'Land of Promise.' I found that hard to believe, considering they had just suffered such a long journey on a boat and might have been simply too worn out to climb the stairs. Some had huddled below deck in deplorable conditions and were now being sent home because they could not climb the 'Golden Steps.' Other ports of entry were Charleston, South Carolina; Galveston, Texas and San Francisco, California, and a few more. I wonder if they had similar unfair requirements?

Once settled, most immigrants looked for work. There were never enough jobs and many employers took unfair advantage of these immigrants. Social tensions were also part of the immigrant experience. Often stereotyped and discriminated against, many immigrants suffered verbal and physical abuse because they were perceived as 'different.' While large-scale immigration precipitated many social tensions, it also produced a new vitality in the cities and states in which immigrants settled. The newcomers helped transform American society and culture, demonstrating that diversity is a source of national strength.

However, to this day, Blacks, women, Asians, and Jews are still looked upon by some Americans as not being entitled to be full participants in this nation. There have been great strides over the centuries to counter discrimination, but it persists, and I believe threatens our unity as a great nation.

THE GOOD

CHAPTER 2: AMERICA THE BEAUTIFUL

I am proud to be an American. Patriotism is a hallmark of my beliefs. I also believe if each of us does the right thing for our country, then everyone benefits.

This country has the most beautiful and wondrous geographic treasures. As I traveled around the world, seeking new horizons, I recognized that America measures high among the world's countries, with a vast confluence of fantastic sights and places.

Most prominent for me are our National Parks, which are spread over the entire country, on the mainland, and beyond. Let's start our journey together by exploring America's greatest gift, our natural beauty.

The largest volcano in America is on the Big Island of Hawaii. Mauna Loa spans 75 miles across the island, taking up approximately one-half of the Big Island. It is the largest active volcano on earth. Mauna Loa is so massive that it continues to sink deeper beneath the ocean under its own weight. With each eruption, the flowing lava, when it reaches the shoreline, adds land mass, increasing the size of the island. That's how Hawaii was born.

When my husband, Paul, and I visited the island, in 1981, we stayed at a hotel near the precipice of the volcano. We could look out the window and there it was. This was at Volcanoes National Park. Thankfully, Mauna Loa had been inactive for many, many, years. But in 1983, the volcano awoke and erupted. It had been inactive until now, 40 years later. I'm sure the hotel is no longer there. The volcano is a powerful force of nature with which humans on the island have learned to live.

Interestingly, the city of Hilo, which is east of Volcanoes National Park, and approximately an hour's drive away by car from Mauna Loa, gets an enormous amount of rain annually. When we were there, we saw that the leaves on the bushes were huge from soaking up all that moisture. At the other end of the island, also about an hour away by car, lies a desert. The city there is called Kona, and near it are black sand beaches, presumably created by the volcano. On this one island, the residents learn to live in an environment with many dimensions. It is the diversity created by the volcano that makes Hawaii what it is. What it can be.

On our mainland, we have Yellowstone, the first government-designated National Park. On

March 1, 1872, President Grant signed the bill into law, establishing the Yellowstone region as a public park, a significant conservation precedent. The park is massive, stretching from Utah into Montana and parts of Idaho. It is well known for its geysers, especially Old Faithful, which erupts on average every 74 minutes, 20 times a day. You can check in at the Park Ranger's office to get the predicted times and be there to watch the eruption. It is quite a sight, shooting up sometimes as high as 180 feet. It is another example of our diverse land.

The most colorful park is Bryce Canyon, located in Southwestern Utah. Despite its name, it's not a canyon. It is a collection of natural amphitheaters, geological structures called "hoodoos" that range up to 200 feet high. Formed by frost, weathering, and the erosion of the river and lakebed sedimentary rocks, the red, orange, and white rocks make up this natural wonder and provide spectacular views. It is the mix of colors that sets this park apart and gives it such power.

The Grand Canyon in Arizona is 277 miles in length, up to 18 miles wide, and attains a depth of over a mile. The Colorado river and its tributaries cut their channels through layer after layer of rock, while lifting the Colorado Plateau. Visitors may take donkeys down to the bottom and may even camp overnight there. Recently, a platform was built reaching out over the canyon with a glass base that you can see through to take in all the splendor. Most visitors prefer the South Rim for viewing. But whether you fly over the massive canyon, drive, or take the train, the view from the rim is spectacular. You just stand there, look out, and try to absorb how "grand" it really is.

The first time we flew in from Las Vegas, the wind buffeting our small plane, made me anxious. It reminded me of how small we are in the context of nature.

The second time we visited the Canyon, we took a train from Williams, Arizona. Only a few centuries ago, it was the embarkation point and route into the canyon. We were in Williams for an Elder hostel program. The town had been a 'honky-tonk' kind of place a century ago, complete with gambling and houses of ill repute for the pleasure of those who visited.. When we were there in the 1980s, the trains had begun operating again and provided easy access to the canyon's South Rim. They even reenacted a train robbery as a stunt, for our entertainment. Times change and people adapt. America has changed, but are we adapting?

We sometimes take things for granted, thinking they were always here. It is hard to believe that it was only in 1957 that President Eisenhower signed the Interstate Highway System into law, and suddenly freeways were under construction all over our country. Most notable was Interstate 40 which crossed the country from East to West.

Previously, we had Route 66, which crossed the country, and gave rise to the song, "I get my kicks, on Route 66." America, with its new highway system, was on the move. This amazing land was opening to all of us to explore, enjoy and exploit.

You would love visiting Arches National Park in Utah. It's legendary with more than 2,000 red sandstone arches that make your eyes pop out. Driving is the best way to see the park, but don't stay in the car. The precariously Balanced Rock will make you want to get up close and take a good look. The boulder on top resembles a mushroom cloud and you will wonder how it has remained on its perch for so long. Nature performs wonders in our beautiful America.

Yosemite National Park, is in the central Sierra Nevada of California, about 150 miles East of San Francisco. Designated a World Heritage site in 1984, Yosemite is internationally recognized for its spectacular granite cliffs, waterfalls, and giant sequoia groves. The 1200-square-mile park contains thousands of lakes and ponds, 1600 miles of streams, 800 miles of hiking trails, and 300 miles of roads. Visitors set up camp and enjoy all sorts of recreation. Mountain climbing on Half Dome is a common sport for excellent climbers. I've heard that because it's so high, sometimes climbers sleep on the side of the mountain and wait till morning to continue the climb.

Black bears are abundant in the park. Sadly, they are often involved in conflicts with humans. Some of these result in property damage, and occasionally, injuries to the park's human visitors. Visitor education and bear management efforts have reduced bear-human incidents. Once again, it is humans who must learn to live with the environment.

Yosemite's uniqueness, scenic beauty, and outstanding wilderness features present the majesty and variety of the Sierra Nevada environment, bringing huge numbers of visitors each year. Most enjoy and revere the natural treasures, but some have little appreciation for what nature has gifted us.

As you can see, each of our National Parks are different with diverse features that make for exciting adventures. As a resident on the East coast of the United States all my life, I was amazed at the colors of even the stones in the Western parks. Visiting a shop and seeing slate cut from the mountains, I thought they were painted by artists. I was awed that these colorful masterpieces were natural to the slopes. It was the colors that made them so dazzling. Imagine if they were all the same color, size, and shape.

While you're on the West Coast, you need to visit the Carlsbad Caverns National Park in the Guadalupe Mountains of Southeastern New Mexico. From the visitor center, you can either hike or take the elevator to the great 'show.'

Carlsbad is a limestone cavern of extraordinary beauty with an incredible variety of natural decorations. Its chambers contain stalactites, and stalagmites, ice formations rising up from the floor or down from the ceiling. There are multiple rooms, each with different formations in such different sizes and structures, but all are remarkable in their variety and beauty.

Carlsbad Caverns was established as one of our protected National Parks in 1930. Over the years, explorers have discovered more chambers and the park now contains over 120 caves, with three open to public tours. It is the most famous and fully developed cave system in America.

Coming back to the East, in West-central Kentucky, is Mammoth Cave National Park. It is the longest cave system in the world with more than 420 miles of surveyed passageways and more to be discovered. It was established as a National Park on July 1, 1941, and named a World Heritage Site on October 27, 1981, an International Biosphere Reservation on September 26, 1990, and an International Dark Sky Park on October

28, 2021. It covers many counties with a river, and its tributaries running throughout.

Mammoth Cave developed in thick aged limestone strata capped by a layer of sandstone, which made the system remarkably stable. Ancient human remains and artifacts within the caves are protected by Federal and State laws. Explorers are properly trained not to disturb archaeological evidence, and some areas of the cave remain out of bounds for even seasoned explorers. The story of human beings in Mammoth Cave spans five thousand years.

Several tours are offered and the caves can be seen on lighted visits ranging from one to six hours. Two tours, lit only by visitor-carried paraffin lamps, are popular offerings that make you feel as if you are an early explorer of this incredible natural wonder. The Echo River tour, one of the cave's most famous attractions, took visitors on a boat ride along an underground river. That tour was discontinued for logistic and environmental reasons in the early 1990s. The sensitive ecology had to be protected.

The legend has it that a young boy, in 1797, while hunting, pursued a wounded bear, and the bear turned around and began to chase him. He discovered the cave entrance when he ran inside for protection from the charging bear.

The National Parks are only some of the beautiful features of our land that we're fortunate to still have. I have visited many of them and learned how important it is to treasure our country's natural beauty. There is one wonder that is man-made, human-created, that I want to include because it represents who we have been and what sustains us.

Mount Rushmore National Memorial is centered on a colossal sculpture carved into the granite face of Mount Rushmore in the Black Hills, near Keystone, South Dakota. It was designed and constructed from 1927 to1941. The sculpture features the 60-foot-tall faces of four

United States Presidents: George Washington, Thomas Jefferson, Theodore Roosevelt, and Abraham Lincoln. These four Presidents were chosen to represent our nation's birth, growth, development, and preservation. The memorial park contains 1,278 acres, and the actual height is 5,725 feet. Sometimes referred to as the Shrine Of Democracy, Mount Rushmore attracts more than two million visitors annually.

The best time to see this awe-inspiring site is at night when the lights are turned on and the glow of each head becomes prominent against the dark sky. It is a great example of a human accomplishment made more glorious by its natural environment.

When exploring this wonderful country, you realize there's a lot to see. I've been blessed to visit 47 states and checked out as much of their fascinating sites of interest as I could manage. There is just too much to see.

On Independence Day, 2022, I watched with pride as the festivities unfolded celebrating our nation's birth. In particular, the New York City fireworks were spectacular as each display of pyrotechnics burst against the sky in perfect sync with the music, mostly patriotic of course. It reminded me of the Bicentennial celebration in New York as multiple tall sailing ships from the eighteenth century sailed up the Hudson River. That was quite a sight to behold. Just think of who we are.

America The Beautiful

O beautiful for spacious skies,

For amber waves of grain,

For purple mountain majesties

Above the fruited plain!

America! America!

God shed his grace on thee

And crown thy good with Brotherhood

From sea to shining sea!

O' beautiful for patriot dream,

That sees beyond the years

Thine alabaster cities gleam

Undimmed by human tears.

America! America!

God shed his grace on thee

And crown thy good with

Brotherhood

From sea to shining sea!

Yes, we must sing of America, a land of many beautiful gifts. But our America today still has human flaws that are disturbing and we must not ignore...

THE BAD

CHAPTER 3: NATIVE AMERICANS

In the fifteenth century, when European settlers began to arrive in North America, the continent was richly populated with North American communities. Hundreds of thousands of people lived in a wide range of environments, from shore to shore. Each community, or nation, had its own distinct culture. The centuries that followed the arrival of Europeans were years of tremendous upheaval, as the expansion of settler territory and the founding and growth of the United States, resulted in

Native American communities being relocated, renamed, contained, dispersed, and in some cases, destroyed.

These changes took place over many centuries, each episode marked by its own set of unique circumstances, but with one result. From negotiations and careful planning, to subterfuge and deceit, from declarations of friendship to outright calls for genocide, from disease, starvation, and bloodshed, despite their resistance, and hope in the face of persecution, the decimation of our Native population is a blot on our history. The fate of our indigenous people was driven by the relentless expansion of European settlement and by U.S. Government policies that relegated the Native Americans to secondary status and deprived them of their independence and dignity.

In September 1620, a small ship called the Mayflower left Plymouth, England, carrying 102 passengers. They were an assortment of religious separatists seeking a new home where they could freely practice their faith. Among them were individuals lured by the promise of land ownership and prosperity in the New World. After an uncomfortable and treacherous Atlantic crossing that lasted 66 days, they dropped anchor near the tip of Cape Cod, far north of their intended destination at the mouth of the Hudson River. One month later, the Mayflower crossed Massachusetts Bay, where the Pilgrims, as they are now commonly known, began the work of establishing a village at Plymouth.

Throughout that first brutal winter, most of the colonists remained on board the ship, where they suffered from exposure, scurvy, and outbreaks of contagious disease. Only half of the Mayflower's original passengers and crew lived to see their first New England spring. In March, the remaining settlers moved ashore, where they received an astonishing visit from a member of the Abenaki tribe who greeted them in English.

Several days later, he returned with another Native American, Squanto. a member of the Pawtuxet tribe. He had been kidnapped by an English sea captain and sold into slavery before escaping to London and returning to his homeland on an exploratory expedition. Squanto taught the Pilgrims, weakened by malnutrition and illness, how to cultivate corn, extract sap from maple trees, catch fish in the rivers, and avoid poisonous plants. He also helped the settlers forge an alliance with the Wampanoag, a local tribe. This alliance would endure for more than 50 years and remains one of the sole examples of harmony between European colonists and Native Americans. As you can see, the Indians welcomed these strangers into their midst and treated them as equals to share their land.

In November 1621, after the Pilgrims' first corn harvest proved successful, the Governor organized a celebratory feast. He invited a group of the fledgling colony's Native American allies to share the feast with them. It is now remembered as America's first Thanksgiving.

A little over 200 years ago, President Thomas Jefferson acquired land west of the Mississippi from France. This was known as the Louisiana Purchase. He then authorized Lewis & Clark to make an expedition to the Pacific Ocean to map out the land.

The most widely held and deeply ingrained popular image of Lewis & Clark also happens to be the most serious misconception of their expedition. In that image, the 'great explorers' crossed North America on their own at the start of the nineteenth century, somehow finding their way through an uninhabited wilderness, blazing a trail where no one had ever gone before.

The truth is quite different. The West they crossed was hardly an uninhabited space. Indians were not only inhabiting it, they had been living on it, traveling back and forth across this 'wilderness' for hundreds of generations. And the even harder truth for some to swallow is that without those Indians, Lewis & Clark would never have made it to the Pacific Ocean and back. That central but often forgotten fact is worth restating. If the west had been uninhabited, the Corps of Discovery would not have succeeded. Make no mistake. to a man, the members of the expedition were uncommonly tough, amazingly resourceful, doggedly determined, and supremely courageous. Clark was as good at intuiting and mapping unfamiliar landscapes as any explorer this country had, and Lewis was single-mindedly devoted to this mission. Nonetheless, it was the Indians that helped them who made the difference between success and failure.

The Mandans gave the expedition buffalo meat and corn to survive the fierce North Dakota winter. The Hidatsas gave them information about the uncertain, unmapped, route that awaited them along the Upper Missouri. They provided mileposts the explorers needed to watch for, down to the details of the sound of the Great Falls and a solitary eagle's nest in a cottonwood tree that would assure they were on the right track. Without Shoshone and Salish horses, Lewis and Clark could not have crossed the Bitterroot Mountains. Without the salmon and camas roots offered freely by the Nez Perce, they would not have recovered from near- starvation after emerging from the mountains. The tribes of the arid Columbia Plateau provided them with much-needed food (dogs mostly) on the expedition's way back when game was impossible to find and the men, despite their hunger, refused to eat the salmon teeming in the river. More food and essential information came from the Chinooks and Clatsops who lived along the Pacific Coast.

The two captains understood from the start how crucial Native Americans were to their success. Lewis spent $559.50, nearly one-quarter of the expedition's entire Congressional appropriation, on presents for the Indians: 8 brass kettles, 130 rolls of tobacco, 500 brooches, 12 dozen pocket mirrors, 4,600 sewing needles, 33 pounds of tiny colored beads, silk ribbons and yards of bright colored cloth, tomahawks that doubled as pipes, and much more. This list doesn't include the boxes of Jefferson peace medals provided at no charge by the United States Mint.

Clark certainly understood the importance of the Native Americans to the success of their mission. Every time he sat down around a campfire with an Indian chief and an interpreter, he asked questions about the tributaries of the Missouri and Columbia and about the far-flung terrain he would not get to see with his own eyes. Then as the chief scratched lines in the dirt with lumps of clay to mark mountains, Clark would add that information to the new map of the West he was compiling for President Jefferson.

Sacagawea was the one full-blooded Indian on the expedition. She has become nearly as famous as the two captains. Although her role tends to be over-romanticized, her contribution to the Corps of Discovery's achievement is noteworthy. Their journals show they immediately sensed that she could be the key to getting Shoshone horses once they reached her homeland in the Western mountains. Even after she helped obtain the horses, Sacagawea's role was vital. "The sight of this Indian woman," Clark wrote as they met tribe after tribe on the Columbia, "confirmed to those people of our friendly intentions as no woman ever accompanies a war party of Indians in this quarter."

Along their route, Lewis & Clark encountered many tribes, who though hesitant, agreed to do them no harm. Lewis & Clark had rough edges. So did every Indian they met. They were all human, after all, bringing to every encounter their biases, self-interest, and the weight of their culture.

In their writing, they described the natives as "savages." This term largely applied to the tribes the Captains considered hostile. In addressing each tribe, they spoke of the "great chief of the Seventeen great nations of America, who will become your only father." You can look to him for protection. He will serve you and not deceive you."

On the Indian side of the council fire, the explorers' speeches were convincing them to see that getting the white man's trade goods would make their people's lives easier, more endurable, and in their view, safer. These new white men may have had a bigger boat and a larger contingent of soldiers than the Indians had seen before, but none of the tribes seemed to feel intimidated by the expedition's presence or to be particularly worried about the "seventeen great nations of America" on the far side of the Mississippi. It was more often the Corps of Discovery that felt outnumbered and in need of being on military alert.

From the vantage point of today, it seems easy enough to see where this was heading: a nineteenth century that would be the most chaotic and traumatic in the history of the Indian people of the West. But Lewis & Clark, and the Indians they met, did not have the luxury of foreknowledge. They were simply trying to manage as well as they could, according to their own best judgments. During a journey of two and a half years, the expedition's relations with Indians had its share of suspicion, disagreements, tensions, and misunderstandings on both sides. What stands out is how multidimensional and richly human the encounters were, how earnestly both sides often strove to understand one another even in the most trying circumstances, and finally, just how many friendships were actually forged across the great cultural divide. The sorrow that lingers beyond the success of the Corps of

Discovery is that what both sides did so well, later people were not able to do. In dealing with Native peoples, our nation didn't learn what Lewis and Clark taught themselves. Lewis & Clark went as students; they came back as teachers. We failed to learn the lessons that they learned from interacting with our indigenous cultures. Instead of learning to live together and share the land, the United States sent their soldiers to deceive and destroy.

The era of President Andrew Jackson is often referred to as the new Jacksonian Democracy, but not everyone was included. There was no initiative from Jacksonian Democrats to include women in political life nor to combat slavery. But it was the Native Americans who suffered the most from Andrew Jackson's vision of America. Jackson, both as a military leader and as President, pursued a policy of removing Indian tribes from their ancestral lands. This relocation would make room for settlers and often for speculators who made large profits from the purchase and sale of land.

Jackson's Indian policy caused the President little political trouble because his primary supporters were from the southern and western states, and generally favored a plan to remove all the Indian tribes west of the Mississippi River. While Jackson and other politicians put a very positive and favorable spin on Indian removal in their speeches, the forced migrations were in fact often brutal. There was little the Indians could do to defend themselves. In 1832, a group of about a thousand Sac and Fox Indians led by Chief Black Hawk returned to Illinois, but militia members easily drove them back across the Mississippi. The Seminole resistance in Florida was more formidable, resulting in a war that began under Chief Osceola that lasted into the 1840's.

The Cherokees of Georgia, on the other hand, used legal action to resist. The Cherokee people were by no means frontier 'savages.' By the 1830s they developed their own written language, printed newspapers, and elected leaders to representative government.

When the government of Georgia refused to recognize their autonomy and threatened to seize their lands, the Cherokee took their case to the Supreme Court and won a favorable decision. John Marshall's opinion for the Court majority in Cherokee Nation vs. Georgia was essentially that Georgia had no jurisdiction over the Cherokees and no claim to their lands. But Georgia officials simply ignored the decision, and President Jackson refused to enforce it. Jackson was furious and personally affronted by the Marshall ruling, stating, "Mr. Marshall made his decision. Now let him enforce it." Finally, federal troops came to Georgia to forcibly remove the tribes.

As early as 1831, the army began to push the Choctaws off their lands to march them to Oklahoma. In 1835, some Cherokee leaders agreed to accept Western land and payment in exchange for relocation. With this agreement, the Treaty of New Echota, Jackson had the green light to order Cherokee removal. Other Cherokees, under the leadership of Chief John Ross, resisted until the bitter end. About 20,000 Cherokee were marched westward at gunpoint on the infamous Trail Of Tears. Nearly a quarter perished on the way, with the remainder left to seek survival in a 'foreign land.' The tribe became hopelessly divided as the followers of Ross murdered those who signed the Treaty of New Echota. The forced march became known as the Trail Of Tears for this reason. It is the most sorrowful legacy of the Jacksonian Era.

The Crazy Horse Memorial is a mountain monument under construction on privately held land in the Black Hills, in Custer County, South Dakota. It will depict the Oglala Lakota warrior, Crazy Horse, riding a horse and pointing to his tribal land. The memorial, commissioned by

Henry Standing Bear, a Lakota elder, is being sculpted by Korczak Ziolkowski, a Polish man who worked with the sculptor who built Mount Rushmore. Standing Bear was unsuccessful at getting the original sculptor for Mount Rushmore. His message is clear:

My fellow chiefs and I would like the white man to know that The red man has great heroes also. Crazy Horse was a Native American war leader of the Oglala Lakota. He took up arms against the U.S. Federal Government to fight against encroachments on the territories and way of life of the Lakota people.

Crazy Horse's most famous action was at the Battle of the Little Bighorn. In the Spring of 1868, the Treaty of Fort Laramie was the existing pact between his tribe and the Federal Government. President Andrew Johnson, at that time, promised the Black Hills would belong to the Indians forever. The government broke the treaty. Crazy Horse ranks among the most iconic of Native American tribal leaders and was honored by the U.S. Postal Service in 1982 with a thirteen cent postage stamp that is part of the Great Americans series.

The monument is being carved out of Thunderhead Mountain, on land considered sacred by some Lakota. The final dimensions are larger than each of the Presidents on Mount Rushmore. In fact, when completed, it will become the world's second tallest statue, after the Statue Of Liberty in India. Standing Bear tried to get the sculpture adjacent to Washington and Lincoln on Mount Rushmore because he felt Crazy Horse to be worthy of this honor, but his request was denied. The monument has been in progress since 1948. It is a non-profit undertaking and does not accept federal or state funding. It accepts contributions and charges fees at its visitor centers.

After Ziolkowski died in 1982 at the age of 74, his widow took charge of the project. Her children and some of their grandchildren continue to work on this dream.

How sad that the United States has this indelible stain on its reputation, as a nation that brutally conquered its indigenous native population because of greed and the lust for land. Why couldn't we have shared this beautiful country as Americans as we moved West in search of new homes?

CHAPTER 4: BLACK AMERICANS

Consider the word, slave. For many, its use is limited to dark-skinned African-American people enslaved to work on America's Southern plantations. The word itself, "slave," likely originated as "slav", a term used for captured white Slavic people sold by other Europeans to Arabs as indentured servants during the eighth and ninth centuries. But the roots of slavery go far back. In Biblical history, the Jews were enslaved by an Egyptian Pharaoh well before the arrival of slaves to America. Moses, with God's help, freed the slaves, a story that gave hope to American's enslaved people.

Throughout history, societies around the world forced those they conquered to work without pay as slaves. While skin color had some impact on who would be enslaved, it was not the only determinant with early slavery. Even in America, the earliest 'slaves' came in a variety of skin colors from a variety of countries. Most worked as indentured servants. The key difference between these people and the African slaves was the latter were captives and had no choice about being sent here. They were treated as a sub-human species, inferior to all others

For the Colonial ruling class, African slaves were easy to identify by their dark skin. This factor ultimately made them a more practical investment than their white-skinned and Native American counterparts. Enslaved indigenous people could easily escape and many could blend in with any Native American population they were able to reach. Escaped white indentured servants could blend in even more readily. Limiting the slave population to black-skinned people was deemed a practical solution by slaveowners, but it gave the false impression that American history was a lily-white story

White Americans had names, labels, for other races, but rarely referred to themselves with such labels. This reinforced the idea that the white population were the majority, the norm, 'race-less' and 'ethnicity-less.' In other words, no label was needed if you were white. You did not have to say it because it was a given. For example, when you spoke about an encounter with a white person, you would say something like, "I met the sweetest lady this morning." The term "white" was assumed.

Why do we need to label people by skin color? Have you ever heard newspeople refer to someone as 'white?' For people of color, it is more likely that a label will be applied: "I met the funniest 'black guy' waiting at the bus today." Would you say, "I met the funniest 'white guy?'" Labels come complete with certain narratives and stereotypes. Racial bias plays out in the media and in many areas of American lives.

Race is, and has always been, the way America has sorted and ranked its people in a bitterly divisive humanity-robbing system. The Constitution declares, "All Men Are Created Equal." It is sad that it did not mention equal rights for Blacks or women.

The GI bill was created to help veterans returning home after World War 2, in 1945. How great it was to win the war and come home to a free higher education and the offer of a housing loan. But blacks, though returning GI's, could not take advantage of these programs because they were not accepted in schools and were not welcomed in many neighborhoods. FHA (Federal Housing Authority) at the time, warned developers, one or two non-whites could topple the kind of values necessary to profit from their enterprise.

The chilling reality is that the American dream fell into the laps of millions of Americans, making the GI bill the 'great equalizer' for a wide range of white people, but Americans of color, the one million black GI's who'd risked their lives in the war, were largely excluded. The same GI bill that had given white families a socio-economic rocket boost, left people of color out to dry. This was not freedom for all.

Blacks going back to their homes in the South were treated to the same discrimination that they left behind before they enlisted as soldiers. Even if they were in their uniform, the brave veterans who fought so valiantly, encountered the new enemy, discrimination. In fact, they were more accepted into the communities in Europe than in those in their homeland, the United States. Some chose not to come home.

I met a young man once who told me that when he applied to a college, he wouldn't state his race on the application because he was black. He was accepted because his application demonstrated he was worthy. But when he showed up, he said it was a surprise to the college officials that he was Black. This young man, after some previous unfortunate experiences, decided to hide the fact that he was black because he attributed his earlier failures to racism. He said that he was judged by the color of his skin and not by his character or ability. Isn't it sad that he had to conceal what makes him so special?

Inequality still persists and discrimination still hurts others. Once, I read a story that illustrates this. I'd like to share it with you.

Marie's daughter, Emily, started kindergarten in Cambridge, Massachusetts, where the school's motto is, "Everyone is Different, Everyone Belongs."

This motto owes its origins to the school's longtime principal, Joe Petner, an educator, who happens to be white. He placed at the core of his educational philosophy the inclusion of children with special needs in regular classrooms. He saw to it that all the children worked together, whether white or black. He believed no one is what we call a 'typical learner.' He also said we all have unique learning styles. People's academic, physical, and social abilities are 'variable' and it is wrong to label learning patterns as 'normal' or 'abnormal,' and 'better' or 'worse.'

I believe this fundamental principle would make for more cohesive and productive communities, both in classrooms and beyond. Emily's mother reported that her daughter thrived in this setting where one of the cultural norms was to figure out how to meet individual needs of each student. Students took enormous pride in their ability to tackle challenges, becoming eager problem-solvers attuned to the needs of their various class members. They became conscious of how excluding one individual can compromise the entire group.

These Kindergarteners who had learned 'side-by-side' with diverse students found themselves the following year as first graders split into reading and math groups, along skin color lines. While the white students became increasingly 'jazzed' by school and their rapid progress, the students of color began to show signs of discouragement. By second grade, the social and academic divide was unmistakable, and by third grade, the gap was so stark as to cause Emily to question her memories of kindergarten 'solidarity.' Even this young student realized that once fully-engaged black and brown children were losing their spark, She was upset that she could not understand the forces behind this change. Her hopes of her classmates forming close cross-racial friendships dwindled as she observed what could neither be explained nor ignored. .

In third grade, Emily asked, "Mom? Why is it that the black kids are all in the lower reading groups?" It crushed her mother that her child had noticed this strange phenomenon. To her, all the grouping appeared to be doing was reinforcing racial stereotypes.

By the fourth grade, the white kids dominated the student body, taking on leadership roles, creating clubs, and forming bonds. What Emily was witnessing, without being aware, was that the white kids were 'deepening' their friendships through white-associated roles and white-oriented subjects. They had come to dominate the life of the classroom. It had become a white school culture. She could see now how effortlessly the cycle of white domination can creep into young lives generation after generation. A pattern emerged of white achievement alongside black and brown withdrawal. She also noted seeing black boys sitting on a bench in the principal's office as a nearly daily occurrence. The boys' facial expressions ranging from detachment to rage, made her recall her urge to blame the boys and their parents for not taking school more seriously and not working to prove commonly held black stereotypes were wrong. She tried not to make a judgment, but she wondered why these boys were there.

The insidiousness of discrimination alarmed a young child. I relate this story to point out how behavior in these classrooms impacted and intimidated the Black children. They no longer felt they were equal, but instead, believed themselves unworthy. This story should alarm all of us.

The disparities appear in many places we may not commonly think about. White people have better access to America's goods and services. People of color feel disenchanted by the lack of opportunities they see offered to whites. They see their peers ending up with low-level jobs or getting into trouble. Too many Blacks see themselves shut out of what most of us think of as the American dream. They assume the attitude that they can't compete in the white-dominated world to raise their social status simply because of the color of their skin.

Neighborhoods throughout this country seem to separate into ethnic or cultural groups. In black neighborhoods, income may be lower, so funding for public services is often also lower. Schools in predominantly black communities may not have the resources to educate their students. Black children often feel unfairly treated by the schools. They may take out their frustration by acting out in class, and other negative behaviors. Some will, unfortunately, seek approval by joining gangs. Many may end up getting into trouble, some ultimately landing in jail. The prisons have a large population of black prisoners, disproportionate to their number in our nation. To add to the vicious circle, families often split due to the many stresses they may face. Mothers end up raising children alone partly because many fathers may simply give up and move out. The black male faces what seem to be insurmountable responsibilities. In too many cases, there are no father figures for youth to emulate. It becomes an endless cycle.

In the South, black maids were allowed into a home, but most weren't allowed to use the bathroom. Many were required to use an outhouse instead. As a child, up North, where I lived, I didn't know discrimination still raised its ugly head. I did not know most country clubs would not allow blacks and Jews into their midst. Sammy Davis, Jr., a well-known entertainer in many clubs, even at the highly-rated Copacabana, wasn't allowed to stay at the hotel. Frank Sinatra, who put together the famous "Rat Pack," welcomed Sammy into his group. He made sure that Sammy Davis was treated the same as the rest of the group. Why didn't the rest of us do that?

The state of racism in America is a brewing toxic stew. It allows anger and mistrust to fester between groups of people. It promises an endless cycle of division in which each group can affirm negative narratives about each other, keeping us in a self-destructive holding pattern. People treated in this way become angry for good reason. They deserve to be heard, which is why it's important to open up the channels for communication. We all need to listen, not with anger. Sometimes, we may hear things that we don't like. Rather than yelling-down the speaker, we need to 'agree to disagree.' We must make a concerted effort to understand each other's beliefs and to accept them.

In contrast to the negative stereotypes many whites may have of Blacks, given the opportunity, many Blacks have risen above the turmoil and the lack of concern for their needs. Yes, they've excelled in sports, but many have become officials in government eager to effectuate change. Blacks have been elected as Mayors, Governors, and Military leaders. They have reached high levels in education, many going on to become instructors and Principals in schools, role models for black pupils who for too long lacked them. On TV, they are visible as news anchors, reporters and actors in top-rated series. Change is happening but many argue it has taken too long. Some say more drastic measures are needed.

Dr. Martin Luther King, Jr. had the highest respect from his Black breathren, but also succeeded in making many white people care about righting the wrongs. He was also able to have an impact on government officials. His concept of the "Beloved Community," a vision of complete racial, class, and national integration and brotherhood, reflected a deep love of the human family and a desire for everyone to thrive as equals. His "I have a dream speech," is the symbol of what we must still strive to achieve.

Thurgood Marshall was a lawyer and civil rights activist, who served as an Associate Justice of the Supreme Court from October 1967 to October 1991. He was the first black man to serve as a Supreme Court Justice. Marshall's parents instilled in him an appreciation for the U.S. Constitution and the rule of law. At a time when many resisted sharing civil rights with non-whites, he risked his reputation and career to make equal rights more than just a meaningless phrase. Because of his courage, men like Clarence Thomas, now in that position, have opportunities long denied to our fellow citizens of color.

The recent movie, *Hidden Figures*, was the moving, mostly unknown, story of female African-American mathematicians who served a vital role in NASA during the early years of the U.S. Space program. Their names were Katherine Johnson, Dorothy Vaughn, and Mary Johnson. Most people had never heard of them until this movie. They were doing research at

Langley Research Center in Hampton, VA, with incredible skills in analytic geometry. Despite their genius and contributions to the space program, they encountered prejudice and discrimination from their colleagues and administrators and their story was kept a secret. When they had a meeting with the Mercury 7 astronauts, John Glenn went out of his way to thank them for their expertise and contributions. When you see the movie, it is sad to witness how these remarkable minds were treated simply because of their skin color.

I think about the 2008 election of President Obama, our first President of color. The elation and hope many felt on election night and Inauguration Day quickly gave way to expressions of fear by some white people behaving as if an invader had taken over the White House. President Obama's skin color allowed his opponents to go from political disagreement to racial bullying. I watched in horror as anti-Obama factions sought to focus only on the fact that he was a "black man," and not on his qualities and character. Rather than uniting to support our leader, tragic pieces of white American hate resurfaced, reigniting racial tensions. Many Republicans spread the belief that he was not an American and demanded proof of his birth, a requirement for election. A New York tabloid cartoon portrayed the President as a monkey. The Mayor of Los Alamitos, California, broadcast an e-mail entitled, "No Easter Egg Hunt This Year," with an illustration depicting the White House lawn covered in watermelons. As this mockery incited white anxiety across the country, ammunition stores found themselves barely able to keep up with the demand. Fear begets fear.

As I said, fear begets fear. Instead of uniting the people of the United States into a "more perfect union," the election of President Barack Obama, through no fault of his own, served as a reminder of how deep in our waters the fear of others still runs.

And Blacks are still harassed by police and
shot in numbers disproportionate to their white
counterparts.

CHAPTER 5: ASIAN AMERICANS

E ven though a handful of Chinese came to our shores by the early part of the nineteenth century, they played a significant role as sailors and merchants. There were many more that came in the mid 1800's. Let's take a look at the history of Asians coming to America in the 1850's. They were eager to escape the economic chaos in China. The money to fund their journey was mostly borrowed from relatives, district associations, or commercial merchants.

Many of these Chinese laborers received news of the deposits of gold found in California. Most, single men, came to try their luck at the California gold rush in 1850. Because archaic conditions existed in the gold fields, the robbery by European miners of Chinese mining area permits was barely pursued or prosecuted. The Chinese gold seekers were often victims of violent assaults.

In response to this hostile situation, these Chinese miners developed an approach that differed from European gold miners. While the Europeans mostly worked as individuals or in small groups, the Chinese formed large teams, which protected them from the attacks, and because of good organization, often gave them a higher yield.

White miners began to resent the Chinese, feeling that they were discovering gold that white miners deserved. Protests ensued with growing discrimination.

When the gold rush ended, Chinese Americans were considered cheap labor. They found employment as farmhands, gardeners, domestics, laundry workers, and most famously, as railroad workers. In the 1860's, it was the Chinese who built the Transcontinental Railroad.

By the 1870's, there was widespread economic depression in America and jobs became scarce. Anti-Chinese resentment grew as Chinese laborers became successful. They suffered increasing racial discrimination. They were called the 'Yellow Peril' at every level of society.

With hostility growing, things got so bad that Congress passed the Chinese Exclusion Act in 1882 virtually banning all Chinese immigration to the United States. It was only in 1943, when China became America's ally in World War II, that Congress finally repealed this discriminatory legislation. Even then Chinese immigrants were limited to a mere 105 people a year.

The Chinese had developed close networks of extended family unions, clan associations and guilds, where their people had a duty to protect and help each other. These units helped new immigrants to relocate, socialize, receive monetary aid, and raise their voices in community affairs.

After the gold rush wound down in the 1860's, the majority of the Chinese work force found jobs in the railroad industry. Chinese labor was integral to the construction of the First Transcontinental Railroad, which linked the railway network of the Eastern United States with California on the Pacific coast. Construction began in 1863 at the two opposing terminal points of Omaha, Nebraska, and Sacramento, California. The two sections merged and were ceremoniously completed on May 10, 1869 with the famous Golden Spike event held at Promontory Summit, Utah. This incredible feat created a nationwide mechanized transportation network that revolutionized the population and economic growth of the American West. The wagon trains of previous decades become obsolete as a modern transportation system took over. The well-organized Chinese teams turned out to be the highly industrious and exceedingly efficient builders that made travel across America much easier.

In California, white landowners began in the 1860's to put thousands of Chinese migrants to work in their large scale farms and other agricultural enterprises. Many of these Chinese laborers were experienced farmers to whose vital expertise the California fruit, vegetable, and wine industries owe much to this very day. Despite their invaluable contributions, Chinese immigrants could not own land due to the restrictive laws in California at the time. Deprived of the ownership rights, they frequently pursued agricultural work under leases or profit-sharing contracts with white employers.

Many of these men came from the Pearl River Delta Region in southern China. There they had learned to develop farmland in largely inaccessible river valleys. This know-how was used for the reclamation of the extensive valleys of the Sacramento San Joaquin River Delta in California.

During the 1870's, before they were excluded, thousands of Chinese laborers that already lived in America played an indispensable role in the construction of a vast network of earthen levees (embankments designed to prevent the flooding of a river) in that region. These workers were used to construct hundreds of miles of levees throughout the delta's waterways in an effort to reclaim and preserve farmland and control flooding. These levees opened up thousands of acres of highly fertile marshlands to agricultural production.

When I was in China, I saw how the farmers grew crops on the sides of mountains. There were terraces of earth all seeded. When they blossomed, the terraces were filled with vegetables and ablaze with color. It was impressive.

As you can see, the ingenuity and organizational skills, their work ethic, and the resourcefulness of the Chinese, played a vital role in the development of our country. It is too bad that because of racial discrimination, the government chose to not allow any more immigration of the Chinese in 1882.

The first Chinatowns appeared in U.S. Cities as far back as 1900. Today, the largest Chinatown in the United States is in New York City, where almost 100,000 Chinese live and work. The second largest is in San Francisco. These towns sprang up to protect the Chinese immigrants from the hate they often encountered. They helped preserve Chinese identity and culture.

Other Asians found their way to our shores, but restricted by the Chinese Exclusion Act, they had to navigate immigration in alternate ways.

Still small numbers filtered in. Many Koreans went to Hawaii which was not part of the United States and was closer than mainland America. Many Indians migrated to Canada and ultimately migrated down to the United States. Filipinos began to arrive after the Spanish-American War in 1898 when the United States annexed the Philippines.

These Asians still had to deal with discrimination. When World War II began, Japanese citizens were placed in internment camps. Many remained there until the end of the war. The government feared they would spy for the Japanese enemy. For many Americans today, these camps are considered one of the saddest episodes in our history.

After the Vietnam war, many Vietnamese immigrated to the United States, and made important contributions to our nation.

In January 1910, the immigration station, Angel Island, opened in San Francisco. It served as the country's major port of entry for Asian immigrants. Known as the Ellis Island of the West, located 6 miles off the San Francisco coast, immigrants without proper documentation were quarantined there for days, or years. It was described as a prison-like environment, according to the National Parks Service. It closed in 1940. I find this disturbing, because I've always believed in immigration.

In 1965, President Lyndon Johnson signed the Immigration & Nationality Act into law. It put an end to immigration policies based on ethnicity and race and ended all Federal quota systems. The result was a wave of Asian immigrants who had been barred from entry to the land of liberty by restrictive laws based on racial discrimination against Asians.

Despite all the hatred, exclusion, and discrimination, Asians faced, they persevered. There were many families that settled in small and larger towns who established grocery stores and other businesses. These were businesses that they were familiar with in order to succeed. Driving down the streets in Edison, New Jersey, you might see Indian restaurants, a Hindu temple, or a mosque. Edison with a population of more than 100,000, is 48 percent Asian. They were attracted to Edison's schools, ethnic grocery stores, and even funeral parlors that know the customs of the immigrant population.

President McKinley, in 1903, signed a program whose larger goal was "benevolent assimilation." His successor, Theodore Roosevelt continued this program after McKinley was assassinated. The competitive grant offered education and advancement opportunities, particularly in the fields of administration, medicine and engineering. This was a positive program to encourage and accept immigrants into our country and help them adapt to their new country.

Family sponsorship was the most common pathway through which Asian immigrants arrive in the United States. In 2010, 36% of new immigrants came from Asia. Up against major confrontations, they thrive. With what they've been able to offer Americans, they should receive acceptance. We are a nation of immigrants.

Education is a priority of Asian Americans. As a group, Asian Americans hold high levels of education compared to the general population: 49% of Asian adults, age 25 or older, hold college degrees. Many do extremely well in their classrooms. Notably, Asian students become their school valedictorians. Asians are winners year after year in the National Spelling Bee. Their family focus on education propels them to the top of their classes. We are fortunate that many devote their lives as doctors and other medical practitioners and researchers.

CHAPTER 6: THE JEWS

The Jewish population in Spain were a formidable group for centuries until Queen Isabella ascended to the throne. With her husband, King Ferdinand, they decided that all the Jews must convert to Catholicism. In 1492, they issued a decree that the Jews must convert or leave the country. This time of terror was called the Spanish Inquisition. The royal decree gave them 4 months to either convert to Christianity or leave. If they did not leave by the deadline, the punishment was execution. Interestingly, this was around the time of Christopher Columbus who set out on his journey to find India. Ironically, much of the funding for this endeavor was from a Jewish nobleman.

So, the expulsion began. Jews found their way to Portugal and The Netherlands, and to other countries that would accept them. Some went to the Western hemisphere.

When my husband and I took a tour of Mexico, our guide, Carlos, told us his family, who had been Jewish, were forced to leave Spain during the Inquisition. They ended up in Mexico, and because of their fear of being persecuted, became Catholics. Some of his family remained Jewish, but he was brought up as a Christian. When we told him that we were Jewish, he hugged me, as if I was family to him. He said we were 'mishpuchah,' which is Yiddish for family.

After the inquisition in Spain, as Jews were dispersed, many came to North America where they found new homes. Some were participants in the American Revolution. One of the most famous was Hyam Solomon, a successful businessman, who became a major financier of the revolution.

President George Washington, remembering the Jewish contribution, wrote a letter in 1790 to the Newport, Rhode Island congregation, the first synagogue at the time. It stated, "May the children of the stock of Abraham who dwell in the land, sit safely under his own vine, and there shall be none to make him afraid." This was reminiscent of a passage from the Bible and appeared to offer protection for Jews in America.

.

Yet there were legal restrictions in many states that prevented non-Christians from holding public office and voting at that time. In 1791, the Bill Of Rights attempted to eliminate those restrictions. After the passage of the Bill of Rights, it was believed that Jews would go from merely being tolerated to full civil and political equality because of their participation in the American Revolution. It was hoped that this would help ensure that antisemitism would never become as common as in Europe. Yet there were always problems with anti-Jewish hate rising to the surface.

Education for Jews was also a primary goal for their families. They gathered their communities together, and established organizations to represent them as a minority.

Jews participated in the Civil War, many in leadership roles. Several Jewish bankers played key roles in providing government financing as well as fighting for the Union.

As Jews moved West after the gold rush, they felt creative freedom in western society, unburdening them from past traditions and opening up new opportunities. Entrepreneurship, philanthropy, and civic leadership became their avenues of involvement in society. Regardless of their national origin, many early Jewish settlers worked as peddlers, later establishing themselves as merchants. The most popular trade was in clothing, followed by small-scale manufacturing and general retailing. Levi Strauss started as a wholesaler dealing with clothing, bedding, and notions. By 1873, he introduced blue jeans, an immediate hit for miners which eventually became popular as informal urban wear. It was also the Jews who founded the famous garment industry centered in New York.

A large majority of Jewish immigration to America began in the late 1800's originating from Eastern Europe. Religious persecution of Eastern European Jews became significantly more pronounced after 1881, following the assassination of Czar Alexander II in that same year. Government-sponsored pogroms in Russia were organized and resulted in much widespread fear and many deaths. Laws were passed that severely restricted Jewish residency along with education and occupational opportunities. The outbreak of the Russo-Japanese War in 1904, forced many Jews to leave Europe to avoid conscription into the army. Russia, while denying her Jewish subjects civil rights, did not object to sending them to Manchuria to stop Japanese bullets.

These and many more reasons propelled Jews to seek refuge in a new country. By 1906, nearly 150,000 Jewish immigrants were settled in New York City's lower East side. In 1930, increasing antisemitism in the United States led to restrictions on Jewish life because of the depression. Whenever problems arise in this country, especially economic issues, Jews are blamed. These restrictions were mostly not legislated but impacted the Jewish presence in various universities, professions and high-end housing communities. Jews were not allowed the freedoms they hoped for.

In the early twentieth century, Los Angeles became the second-largest Jewish base in the U.S.. The most dramatic cast of characters were in a place called Hollywood. Some Jews, frustrated with discrimination in the East, found their way to Los Angeles and started the movie industry. MGM, Paramount, Warner Brothers, and others, were all initiated by Jewish men. Their guiding belief was that if they could not be accepted in other areas, they would start their own new ventures. And, of course, the rest is history.

Another great example of Jewish entrepreneurship was Julius Rosenfeld. He transformed a small mail-order business into Sears Roebuck, at one time, the largest retailer in America. His catalog brought an unprecedented variety of goods to the most remote and rural parts of America. When I visited Kanab, Utah, I was able to see the first house built entirely by using the Sears Roebuck catalog as its plan and sole source of supplies.

The SS St. Louis sailed from Germany in May 1939, carrying 936 Jewish refugees fleeing Hitler. Not allowed to dock in Cuba, it was also refused permission to unload in the United

States by order of President Roosevelt as the ship waited in the Caribbean Sea between Florida and Cuba. Initially, Roosevelt showed a limited willingness to take in some of those on board. But the Immigration Act of 1924 made that illegal and much public opinion was strongly opposed. Unable to get approval, the ship returned to Europe. Some fortunate passengers were allowed to remain in Great Britain. Eventually, 620 of the passengers were accepted in various European nations. Of these, only 278 survived the Holocaust, Germany's murder of 6 million Jews, approximately two-thirds of the Jewish population of Europe.

These tight U.S. immigration laws were not lifted during the Holocaust. News began to reach the U.S. in 1942 of the extermination of Jews by the Nazis. Still, little was done. It has been estimated that approximately 200,000 Jewish lives could have been saved had it not been for the bureaucratic obstacles to immigration deliberately created.

In 1965, President Johnson signed the Immigration & Nationality Act, which eliminated a long-standing quota system that helped lead to a significant increase in the number of regions of origin for immigrants to the United States. Even in 2021, laws requiring the teaching of the Holocaust in middle schools are only on the books in 16 states.

500,000 Jewish Americans fought in World War II, yet antisemitism continued to be widespread in America throughout the first half of the Twentieth century. The Anti-Defamation League was formed to deal with antisemitic incidents. It is still active today because anti-Jewish hate and violent incidents continue to be a major problem. Jews were discriminated against in some fields of employment. They were not allowed to stay in some resort areas. Their enrollment at colleges was limited by quotas. In response, Jews established their own country clubs, resorts, and universities, such as Brandeis in Massachusetts.

Some hotels and resorts refused to accept Jews. This led to Jews creating alternatives. The famous 'Borscht Belt' resorts were established in the Catskill mountains of upstate New York. The name comes from borscht, a soup of Ukrainian origin, made with beets as the main ingredient. It was brought by Jewish immigrants to the U.S. The name is a play on colloquial names from other American regions such as the "Bible Belt." In its heyday as many as 500 resorts catered to guests of various incomes. These resorts, built from 1920 to the 60s, ranged from bungalow colonies to expansive hotels. Some major resorts, such as the Concord Hotel, stayed open until 1998. Clients came mainly from the New York City and New Jersey areas seeking a break from urban life. The increased popularity of air travel and other factors caused the younger generation to choose more exotic destinations.

At these hotels, food was of great importance. There was a sense that 'too much was not enough,' and people gorged themselves with the opportunity to ask for seconds. Husbands traveled back to the city because they had to go to work. Often, they took 'doggy bags' with them. Nobody went hungry in the Borscht Belt.

The hotels and resorts became a 'cradle' of American Jewish comedy. Since the 1920s, the Borscht Belt entertainment circuit helped launch the careers of many famous comedians. Those who got their start and regularly performed in the hotels included such famous performers as Woody Allen, Milton Berle, Mel Brooks,

George Burns, Phyllis Diller, Danny Kaye, Alan King, Jerry Lewis, Jackie Mason, Joan Rivers, Alan Sherman, and many more.

Some of the humor became legendary. As an example, Henny Youngman joked, "My doctor said I was in terrible shape. I told him I want a second opinion." He replied, "OK, you're ugly too." "After surgery, I asked, "will I be able to dance?" The doctor replied, "Yes." I said, "Oh good, I never danced before." It was humor based on life. There was little need for 'off-color' jokes. They were just funny.

These resorts have been immortalized as the setting for the movie, "Dirty Dancing." Several episodes of "The Marvelous Mrs. Maisel" are set in the Catskills and depict Catskill resort living in nostalgic detail. But all the Jewish resorts are gone now. People have found other places to travel. It was a wonderful place to feel comfortable as Jews.

In central New Jersey, where my husband and I bought our first house, our new Reform Temple Rabbi suggested an outreach program with a local Catholic church. These religious leaders exchanged pulpits, learning from each other's beliefs, rituals and even sermons. As the Social Action chairman, I decided to form interfaith dialogue groups which were highly successful. I was in charge of the program. In our group of three Jewish couples and three Catholic couples, we stated at the outset, "we are not here to change each other's minds, but to accept our differences." That should be the guiding principle of all Americans.

In Tampa, where we lived from 1982 to 2003, a group of churches and synagogues shared a 'service of thanks' together. They recognized that on Thanksgiving, every religion should be thankful for what we have. I brought that idea to my temple in The Villages and that tradition was a wonderful way to share a holiday. It continued for many years.

There were many well-known Jewish individuals who should be recognized for their contributions to our country. A few examples include:

- Dr. Selman Waksman - discovered Streptomycin.

- Dr. Jonas Salk – identified an injected vaccine to cure Polio

- Dr. Albert Sabin – created an oral vaccine that eradicated Polio from the United States

- Henry Kissinger – presented the 1973 Paris agreement that brought about a ceasefire in the Vietnam War, and the withdrawal of American forces.

- Albert Einstein – A physicist and genius who applied his "Theory of Relativity" to model the structure of the universe.

And many more. The Jewish population of this country is only 2%, but many have made enormous achievements.

We should recognize the contributions of all our immigrant groups and accept individuals from other walks of life. Their hard work and ingenuity have provided momentous enhancements to all of our lives. We should never forget what we've achieved from their expertise and offer them the respect and equal rights from which we will all benefit.

CHAPTER 7: WOMEN

Though women in our nation have been treated as second-class citizens in earlier times, there were always those who took the 'bull by the horn' and fought for independence and equality. Women have been many things other than housewives: only two examples are Harriet Tubman who worked with the Underground Railway to free slaves and Susan B. Anthony who led the fight for women's right to vote.

Beginning in the mid-nineteenth century, several generations of women became suffrage activists. They lectured, wrote, marched, lobbied, and practiced civil disobedience to achieve what many Americans considered a radical change in the constitution. Their goal was to guarantee all women the right to vote. Sometimes, the suffragettes were forced to use more confrontational tactics such as picketing, silent vigils, and hunger strikes. It took courage to stand up for their rights.

In July 1848, Elizabeth Cody Stanton and Lucretia Mott organized the first women's rights convention in Seneca Falls, N.Y. The convention produced a list of demands called the Declaration Of Sentiments. Modeled after the Declaration Of Independence, it called for broader educational and professional opportunities for women and the right of married women to control their wages and property. Little substantial change resulted from the Declaration through 1920. After this historic gathering, women's voting rights became a central issue in the emerging debate about women's rights in the United States.

In 1869, the National Women Suffrage Association with Stanton and Anthony was formed, and the struggle to gain the right to vote began in earnest. It did not come easily. Susan B. Anthony was charged with "wrongful and unlawfully" voting in the 1872 election in Rochester, N.Y., simply because she was a person of the female sex. She was one of several women arrested for illegally voting at that time.

In the second decade of the twentieth century, women suffragists began staging largely-attended and dramatic parades to draw attention to their cause. In 1913, more than 5000 suffragists from around the country paraded down Pennsylvania Avenue in Washington D.C..

A resolution was proposed by the suffragists in 1916 stating: "the women of Australia, New Zealand, a part of Canada, and several important European countries, now vote on equal terms with men. The disenfranchised women of the

United States are as intelligent, law-abiding, and patriotic as any women of the world."

In 1917, the first White House picketing by this group took place. They hadn't picketed at the White House before. The participants stood vigil at the White House itself, demonstrating in silence six days a week for nearly three years. The 'silent sentinels' let banners comparing President Woodrow Wilson to Kaiser Wilhelm of Germany, speak for them. Many were arrested and jailed in deplorable conditions. Some of these incarcerated women went on hunger strikes and had to endure forced feedings. Their treatment by the government gained great sympathy for women's suffrage and the courts later dismissed all charges against them.

When New York adopted woman suffrage in 1917, and Woodrow Wilson changed his position to support an amendment in 1918, the political balance began to shift in favor of granting the vote to women. There was still strong opposition to enfranchising them and petitions from anti-suffrage groups. Eventually, the suffragists won the political support necessary for ratification of the Nineteenth Amendment to the Constitution. For 42 years, the measure had been introduced at every session of Congress, but either ignored or voted down. The work of the suffragists finally resulted in it being debated in Congress in 1919. In May, 1920, Congress voted for its approval. Women had fought long and hard and finally, were able to vote, a major milestone.

Amelia Earhart was an American aviation pioneer and writer. During an attempt at becoming the first woman to complete a circumnavigational flight of the globe in 1937, Earhart and navigator Fred Noonan disappeared in the central Pacific Ocean, near Howland Island. The two were last seen on July 2, in New Guinea, one of the final legs of the flight. They presumably died in the Pacific and were declared dead on July 5, 1939. Earhart was

three weeks short of her fortieth birthday and
had already been the first female aviator to fly
solo, non-stop, across the Atlantic Ocean in
1932.. She set many other records, promoting
commercial air travel, and writing best-selling
books about her flying experiences. Known as
one of the most inspirational American figures
in aviation from the late 1920s and throughout
the 1930s. She is often compared to the early
aeronautical career of aviation pioneer, Charles
Lindbergh. Investigations and public interest in
her disappearance continues more than eighty
years later. (I took a class recently about her and
the theory was that she and Noonan crashed
and were captured by the Japanese.) Whatever
happened can never erase her legacy as a woman
who excelled in what was then a man's sky.

During World War II, American women took
jobs in the military and defense industry, as men
went off to fight in the war. The war provided
unprecedented opportunities for women to enter

into jobs that had never before been open to women, particularly in the defense industry. They faced challenges in overcoming cultural stereotypes against working women as well as finding adequate childcare during working hours. Previously, they had been restricted to "traditionally female" professions such as typing and sewing, and most women were expected to leave the workforce as soon as they had children, if not as soon as they married.

From 1940 to 1945, 5 million women entered the workforce, taking jobs in defense plants and factories around the country. In the aircraft industry, the majority of workers were women by 1943.

There was considerable cultural resistance to women going to work in such male dominated environments. In order to recruit women for the factory jobs, the government created a propaganda campaign centered on a figure known as "Rosie The Riveter." Rosie was tough yet feminine. To reassure men that the demands of war would not make women more masculine, some factories gave female employees lessons in how to apply makeup and assured that cosmetics were never rationed during the war. Keeping women 'looking their best' was believed to be important for male morale.

Although women often earned more money than ever before, it still was far less than men received doing the same jobs. Nevertheless, many achieved a degree of financial self-reliance that some found enticing. American women would have found other opportunities without the war since women are strong and can make history just as much as any man can. But when a large number of the male population went off to fight in WW II, this was an unprecedented opportunity for women to prove themselves.

There were significant challenges. Working mothers faced the dual role of childcare and breadwinner. Eleanor Roosevelt urged her husband, President Franklin Delano Roosevelt, to approve the first government childcare facilities act in 1942. Eventually, seven centers, serving 105,000 children were built. The First Lady also urged industry leaders to build model childcare facilities for their workers.

Approximately 350,000 American women joined the military during WW II. They worked as nurses, drove trucks, repaired airplanes, and performed clerical work. Some were killed in combat or captured as prisoners of war. Over 1600 female nurses received various decorations for courage under fire.

Those who joined the Women's Air Force Service Pilots, WASPs, flew planes from factories to military bases. Many women also flocked to work in a variety of civil service jobs. Others worked as chemists and engineers, developing weapons for the war. The latter included thousands of women recruited to work on the Manhattan Project, developing the Atomic Bomb.

Social commentators worried that when men returned from military service, there would be no jobs available for them. They admonished women to return to their "rightful place" in the home as soon as victory was declared. Although as many as 75% of women reported they wanted to continue working after WW II, they were laid off in large numbers at the end of the war. It would have seemed logical that women could still work while their returning veterans took advantage of the GI Bill to continue their education, but many men resisted.

Women's participation in the workforce did bounce back relatively quickly. Despite the stereotype of the "1950s housewife," perpetuated by television programs, by 1950, approximately 32% of women were working outside the home, and about half were married. WW II had solidified the notion that women were in the workforce to stay. (On a personal note: I went to work when I married in 1954, giving up my college studies so that my Korean War veteran husband could use his GI Bill, and continue his education. He supported that decision.)

On June 12, 1948, Congress passed the Women's Armed Services Integration Act signed by President Harry Truman. This Act granted women the right to serve as permanent and regular members in all 4 branches of the military in a number of official capacities but prohibited their full participation in combat. When they were admitted into the military, the men were openly upset because most men didn't think a woman soldier could be equally effective as a male. Ridicule was often joined by harassment, abuse, and sexual assault. It was not easy for women to serve in the military but they persisted.

In 1976, the first females joined the West Point Military Academy. 119 women made history by being admitted to this previously all-male military college. 62 of those women later graduated in 1980, becoming Second Lieutenants. Another barrier was broken.

Many Federal acts followed over the years amending the laws so that women were allowed to reach grades of commander and lieutenant commander.

Janet Wolfenbarger was a graduate of the Air Force Academy in 1980. Throughout her career in the Air Force, she moved up the ranks. In February 2012, President Obama nominated her to be the first woman 4 Star General in the Air Force, and she was confirmed by the Senate in March 2012. She retired in that capacity. In her 3 ½ decades of active duty, she witnessed major changes and great progress in a host of areas for women in the services in all ranks up and down the chain of command.

In the mid-70s, there were still government orders on the books that allowed military services to separate women involuntarily, should they become pregnant, become a mother through adoption, or have a stepchild. Today the services authorize caregiver leave, so women no longer need to choose between a military career and having a family.

Women have been fighting for their rights, not only the right to vote, but to earn respect in careers and the military, and in all areas. In 1966, a group was established called NOW (National Organization for Women). Betty Friedan, its leader, led 28 women in the fight to establish a Women's Bill Of Rights. The founders were frustrated with the way in which the Federal government was not enforcing the new anti-discrimination laws. Employers were still discriminating against women in terms of hiring and giving unequal pay to men. The women believed they needed to form a feminist pressure group. The organization now consists of 500 chapters, the largest has approximately 500,000 members. These dedicated women lobby for gender equality within the existing political system.

Another famous fighter for women's rights was Gloria Steinem, a major advocate who began to publish *MS.* magazine. The first issue came out in 1972. It was intended to be a publication for women whose interests went "beyond the limits of home and husband." It was the first mainstream magazine by and for women.

In 1972, Senator Birch Bayh introduced Title IX, which prohibited discrimination in education based on sex or gender. He said, "there was a stereotype that women are pretty things who go to college to find a husband, or who go on to graduate school because they want to find a more interesting husband, finally marry, have children, and never work again." There were other negative comments. Some colleges had a desire to not waste a "man's place" for the "weaker sex". These ideas, and comments that women were not worthy of an education, held them back.

Title IX is an important step in the effort to provide for women of America, something that is rightfully theirs. It is an equal chance to attend the schools of their choice, to develop the skills they want, and to apply these skills with the knowledge that they have a fair chance to secure jobs of their choice, with equal pay for equal work. Title IX became public law on June 23, 1972. Later, in 1974, Senator Jacob Javits of New York, helped pass an amendment that Title IX guarantees would be applied to sports as well. This amendment was followed by a great increase in the number of females participating in sports.

In 1972, the Equal Rights Amendment (ERA) was a proposed amendment to the U.S. Constitution designed to guarantee equal rights for all American citizens regardless of sex. It sought to end legal restrictions between men and women in divorce, property ownership, employment and other matters. As of now twelve states have not ratified it. Three fourths of the states are needed before it can become law. Current efforts by members of Congress support removing the time limit which appears in the preamble to the Equal Rights Amendment of 1972. Constitutional Legal scholars have stated that Congress has the legal right to officially remove the deadline for passage of the ERA. It must pass in both houses of Congress. Thirty-eight states have voted to ratify the Amendment. It has not yet passed. Hopefully, it will soon.

A major milestone for women took place in 1973 when the Supreme Court ruled in the case of Roe vs. Wade that the Constitution allowed women to get an abortion. This was based on the Due Process clause of the Fourteenth Amendment to the U.S. Constitution which provides a fundamental "right to privacy," that protects a woman's right to abortion. The justices ruled that there could be no restrictions and made abortion legal in all fifty states. Unfortunately, the Supreme Court recently reversed this decision and reverted the authority to the states, a major setback for female rights.

Despite our advances, our fight for equal rights is still not over. We have to continue to stand up and be recognized as equal partners in this country.

THE UGLY

CHAPTER 8: ASSAULT ON OUR COUNTRY

An insurrection that resulted in the attack on our Capitol occurred on January 6, 2021. Almost two centuries before this date was the last time the Capitol was ever attacked. That was on August 24, 1814. It was surreal to witness such an egregious event, an assault on our democratic government.

The historic earlier attack was during the War Of 1812 against the British. In that war, the British descended on Washington, D.C., and set fire to many government buildings. The Capitol

Building, the Supreme Court, and the President's Mansion, the former name of the White House, were in flames. Fortunately, at the Capitol, the building was still being constructed and the architect had used fireproof building materials. As a result, the exterior structure survived, and many of the interior spaces remained intact. However, the city was ablaze in a great bonfire, and it took many years to restore it while using temporary quarters to house the government.

This government has been strong, able to withstand dissidents who believe in overturning what so many Americans fought for. Thankfully, our government survived that regrettable day in January. We are the longest-existing democracy worldwide and will keep fighting anyone or any group who tries to change our democratic system of government. That is why we must unite. January 6, 2021 proved that we must never take our freedoms for granted.

THE HERE AND NOW

There was a documentary on TV of an elephant whose best friend is a dog. Together, they roam and enjoy each other's company every day. When the dog has an injury to its leg and is unable to walk and be with his friend, the elephant just stands by the dog's enclosure and waits day after day. Ultimately, the dog is carried out to meet the elephant. It brings tears to your eyes to see the excitement and happiness the elephant displays when he sees his friend again. With its trunk and its foot, it reaches out to gently touch the dog. This continues every day until the dog is healed and they are together sharing their time. It demonstrates to me that all species can be friends and relish each other's company, and respect each other, though we are all different. Even humans can do this if we try.

As a society, we should share our cultures and understand that we are all Americans. We don't always agree on everything, but we should recognize the right of people to have differences of opinion. We can agree to disagree. Sometimes, we have arguments, and we might end up in a fight with a bloody nose or a black eye, but generally civility reigns. That has changed with the bitterness and divisiveness in our country today. Hate has taken control. If you don't agree with someone, you lash out with insults or a gun. If you don't agree with someone, you send messages of hate: "God will get you." The concept of God was supposed to foster love and peace. How can some people use God to justify hate?

Senseless hate has resulted in multiple incidents of armed attacks, mostly by young men using assault weapons such as AR-15s. These weapons are intended for military use, and not private individuals. It is a disturbing fact, confirmed by CNN consultants that there are more assault weapons (over one million) in the hands of private individuals than in our military.

Tragically, There have been mass shootings in schools such as Columbine High School, Denver, CO, where these mass murder sprees appear to have begun in 2012. Subsequently, these terrifying shootings continued in schools such as Virginia Tech, Sandy Hook Elementary in Newtown, Connecticut, Parkland High in Fort Lauderdale, Florida, Uvalde Elementary in Texas, at a concert in Las Vegas, Nevada, a supermarket in Buffalo, New York, and a parade in Highland Park, Illinois. No place in our nation is immune to hate and these terrible outbursts of gun violence.

At the Tree Of Life synagogue in Pittsburgh, Pennsylvania, eleven worshippers were killed because they were Jewish. There have also been mass shootings in churches. We have reached the point that in my temple, we decided to hire security for every service, event, and large meeting.

Today, we have 'active shooter' rehearsals everywhere. There is a widespread sensation that we're no longer safe anywhere. Each day we wake

up and wonder if our children and grandchildren
are safe to go to school or if we can celebrate a
parade on our Independence Day or any other
time without fear.

Who is to blame? The National Rifle
Association (NRA) won't accept responsibility
or any limits on weapons. The NRA and gun
right organizations blame these attacks on mental
illness, but other countries have individuals
with mental illness and don't have these mass
shootings.

Throughout history, people in power have
ignored and tried to silence entire populations
who cry out against injustice. It's hard work and
dangerous to speak out about some issues, and
even harder to try and change people's minds.
But people in power often believe they do not
have to listen to their constituents. They believe
they have the authority to avoid criticism and the
voice of the people. In a democracy such as ours,

elected representatives have the responsibility to hear opposing views.

Assault weapons are easy to acquire with hardly any restrictions impeding ownership. Congress, in 2022, finally voted on some restrictions, but not enough to stop the tragedies. Many think a complete ban on AR-15s and similar assault weapons is the answer. Democrats in the Senate wanted to approve more restrictions, but they did not have enough votes from Republicans to move it into law. I ask myself what is the thinking of these deniers? Innocent people are dying. Someday, it could be someone in their own family that faces gun violence. Yet they are blinded by politics. I think their refusal to act on gun violence, even to limit the availability of assault weapons, is a dereliction of their oath to protect the citizens of America.

Politics has changed drastically in our country. There have always been Democrats and Republicans, and even Independents. And yes, they believe in different laws and policies, but most often have worked to find compromises. There has been dissension in the past, but ultimately something got resolved because there was a willingness to do what was best for the country. Now, there are no compromises. It is just, "my way or the highway."

In the Senate, in this congress, the Republicans were led by Mitch McConnell. When he was asked by the media, "What's your agenda?" he responded, "To block anything the Biden administration puts forth." That's an agenda? He won't even allow discussion. In the current congress, we had a 50/50 split in the Senate, so not much was accomplished since most votes were along party lines rather than for the benefit of the people. Much of the same went on in the House of Representatives. Aren't these individuals supposed to be representing their constituents?

Politics has even changed discourse among neighbors, friends, and relatives. A barrier has developed that sets limits to civil discussion. Vision is blocked. Conversations are wary. Contacts have been split asunder and some families end up not talking to each other. The climate has changed. I sometimes think of 'climate change' and laws to improve our environment. Do we need a law to change people's behavior? Can we learn to live together again?

In politics, you can vote out bad behavior, which we did when we voted out Donald Trump. He was a President who claimed he knew more than anyone else. Even once claimed he was smarter than Lincoln. To top it off, he tried to stay in power by pulling off an insurrection, just like a "banana republic." What bothers me most is that so many in Congress still follow his rhetoric. They act like vigilantes, and the hate continues.

After the killing of George Floyd in broad daylight, where a small group of police chose to kill a Black man in front of witnesses, I thought that incident would change police conduct. Throughout the following months, protests were conducted in cities and towns all across the country against incidents of police brutality. A large number of Black and white, young and old, citizens together, voiced their anger over this injustice. Statements were made for change by members of Congress. Yet, here we are in 2022, and we still get reports of these kinds of incidents.

It's a harrowing experience to be a female in America. Sexual abuse is rampant, and some men believe they have the power to prey on young girls. Even in the Olympics, some coaches for gymnastics took advantage of the athletes, and there have been a number of sexual abuse cases. There is a lack of trust that hurts the athletes and the reputation of sports. There are also cases where men who can't deal with a woman's accomplishments resort to verbal abuse which ultimately may become sexual assault. There are increasing cases of incest in homes where young girls are especially vulnerable. Children should believe they are safe in their own homes. Sadly, many are too young to know how to protect themselves. We must work harder to educate and protect our children from these predators.

When the Supreme Court overturned Roe vs Wade and banned abortion, the states were given control. In South Dakota, where abortion was completely banned with no exceptions, a ten-year-old girl was impregnated by rape, and forced to carry the child to birth. Indiana intervened and will allow her to get an abortion there. But isn't it incredible that a raped ten-year-old girl must carry the child of her rapist? There has to be some intelligent understanding that rape is a crime, and the victim should not be held responsible if they become pregnant as a result.

Arizona has been allowing abortion since the beginning of the twentieth century, and it's now been banned. Other states may soon follow. Roe vs Wade was the law for almost 50 years and allowed women to "choose," to make a decision for themselves, not have their choices controlled by someone else. There are many reasons women choose to have an abortion. They may feel they are too young. They already have too many children and financial circumstances dictate that they cannot afford to raise a child. Some may be emotionally unstable or have serious medical problems. Many states have instituted a total ban with no exceptions. Some states want to ban abortion after miscarriages and even after a young girl is raped. How restrictive is that? Control, that's the word. The right for the government to have control over a woman's reproductive system is what is at stake.

What about government control over medications? There is discussion by some state governments to not allow the purchase of methotrexate, which is used to overcome the pain of Rheumatoid Arthritis and some cancers. They believe this drug may also stop a pregnancy, so it shouldn't be allowed to be sold. The passage of this ban would put some women in an uncompromising and tragic position. There seem to be no limits to what lawmakers decide a woman's life should be.

Many states and companies have committed to removing barriers the governments have erected against helping women. Some companies provide comprehensive access for reproductive care. Examples of such corporations are Disney, Apple, and Microsoft. If you're an employee and require travel, they will provide financial support to help women employees get to an abortion clinic. At Disney, their benefits cover family planning and pregnancy-related issues: "Disney will continue to prioritize the health, safety, and well-being of our team members and their families," is their statement of policy. But what about all those women whose companies can't or won't supply these services? Shouldn't our government assist them? Shouldn't our representatives strive to reverse this terrible Supreme Court decision that hurts so many Americans, not just women?

Anti-Semitic incidents declined for many years but have reemerged lately. Incidents of swastika drawings appearing on Jewish belongings have been occurring at a number of American universities. The Vasser College Students for Justice in Palestine published a WW II Nazi propaganda poster depicting Jews as part of a monster's body trying to destroy the world. The New York Post recently released the contents of a New York Police Department (NYPD) report that stated the number of antisemitic incidents in the city increased by 35%. In Los Angeles, such incidents increased 48% since 2013. Just in 2014 alone, the Anti-Defamation League (ADL) reported 912 incidents across the U.S. It always seems that when the tide turns in citizens' lives in this country, economically, politically, or socially,

Jews are blamed. I don't understand it, but I am more uneasy as a Jew living in this country than I ever was.

We all have different cultural backgrounds, but we must secure the rights of every American to a decent life and freedom from hate, persecution, and discrimination. We created an America "Of, By, and For the People." We've all been told in scripture to "love thy neighbor as yourself." Too often we've failed to live up to that ideal, our potential, because of irrational fear, jealousy, or resentment. How many haters have become paralyzed and unable to make a necessary change or face a difficult challenge because of their irrational hate? How many of us have received harmful and denigrating messages which cause us to see ourselves as not 'good enough,' unworthy, or inferior? How many of us are afraid to confront the obstacles in our lives because we were bullied or labeled by prejudice and hate?

When we cling to what we know, even if destructive, we walk in circles, never achieving our goals or realizing our dreams. Are we willing to take a leap of faith to embrace change and enter a brighter future? We need to start by joining hands and marching together.

Think of our beautiful America, and what we've been given: "one land indivisible, with liberty and justice for all." Isn't that what we all want? Isn't that worth working for?

AND THE PRIDE...

CHAPTER 9: ONE DOLLAR BILL

D o you know the secret of the dollar bill?

Take out a dollar bill. Look on the back. You will discover a lot of thought went into formulating the common dollar's design.

LET'S TAKE A CLOSER LOOK

On the rear of the One Dollar Bill, you will see two circles. Together, they comprise the Great Seal of the United States. The First Continental Congress requested Benjamin Franklin and a group of men to come up with this seal. Most people don't know it took them four years to accomplish this task and another two years to get it approved. That is how important they felt this seal was for our new nation.

If you look at the left-hand circle, you will see a pyramid. Notice the face is lighted, and the western side is dark. This country was just beginning. We had not begun to explore the west or decided what we could do for Western Civilization. The Pyramid is uncapped, again signifying that we were not even close to being finished. Inside the capstone, you have the 'all-seeing eye,' an ancient symbol for divinity. It was Franklin's belief that one man couldn't do this task alone, but a group of men with the help of God, could do anything.

The Latin above the pyramid says, ANNUIT COEPTIS. Do you know what that means? The translation from the ancient Roman language is, 'God has favored our undertaking.' The

Latin below the pyramid, NOVUS ORDO SECLORUM, means, 'a new order has begun.'

At the base of the pyramid you see MCCCLXXI, the Roman numeral for 1776, the date of the Declaration of Independence. You also can see the words, 'IN GOD WE TRUST' on this currency, a restatement of our founders' faith in a higher power.

The symbols in the right-hand circle appear in every National Cemetery in the United States. For example, it is on the Parade of Flags Walkway at the Bushnell Florida National Cemetery and is the centerpiece symbol of most of our military heroes' monuments. It also appears on the seal of the President of the United States and is always visible whenever he speaks, yet few people know what all these symbols mean.

The most noticeable symbol of America for many is the Bald Eagle. The eagle was selected as a symbol of victory for two reasons: First, he is not afraid of a storm. He is strong and smart enough to soar above it. Secondly, he wears no crown. This was important to our founders because we had just broken away from the King of England and they did not want our nation to become another monarchy ruled by one man.

Notice the shield in front of the eagle. It is unsupported. It looks as if it is floating. This was meant as a statement that this country could now stand on its own. At the top of the shield, you can see a white bar. This signifies Congress, viewed as a unifying factor: we were coming together as a nation. Look in the Eagle's beak and you will read, 'E PLURIBUS UNUM' meaning, 'one from many.' A restatement of the idea that we were uniting.

Above the Eagle, you will see thirteen stars representing the thirteen original colonies, and any clouds of misunderstanding rolling away. Again, a statement that we were coming together as one.

Notice what the Eagle holds in his talons: an olive branch and arrows. The olive branch declares that our country wants peace, but the arrows make it clear we will never be afraid to fight to preserve peace. The Eagle always wants to face the olive branch, but in a time of war, his gaze turns toward the arrows.

Finally, look again at the arrangement of the 13 stars in the right-hand circle. Most people never notice that they are arranged as a Star of David. This arrangement was ordered by George Washington. He had asked Hyam Solomon, a wealthy Philadelphian Jew who helped finance the American War for Independence, what he would like as a personal reward for his services to the Continental Army. Solomon replied that he wanted nothing for himself, but something for his people. The Star of David was the result. Few people know that it was Solomon who saved the Continental Army through his financial contributions. They also don't know that in doing so, he died a pauper.

Many say that the number 13 is unlucky. This is almost a worldwide belief. You will usually never see a room numbered 13, or hotels or motels with a thirteenth floor. But think about this:

- 13 original colonies

- 13 signers of the Declaration Of Independence

- 13 stripes on our flag

- 13 steps on the Pyramid

- 13 letters in, 'Annuit Coeptis'

- 13 letters in 'E Pluribus Unum'

- 13 stars above the Eagle

- 13 bars on that shield

- 13 leaves on the olive branch

- 13 fruits, and if you look closely

- 13 arrows

For an American, 13 was a very important number. It stood for thirteen distinct colonies joining forever as one great nation. Just think of the creativity, perseverance, and strength, it took these men to encapsulate who Americans were and what we stood for and project it on our dollar bill and you understand how important it was then and now for all of us to come together as one.

CHAPTER 10: THE STAR SPANGLED BANNER

We sing "The Star Spangled Banner," as our National Anthem at every major event. It is our song to unite us as Americans, but how many of us ever think about its origin or meaning? Many times, I've wondered why we didn't select "America, The Beautiful," instead, thinking it more closely reflects who we are, and is easier to sing.

Reflecting back to September 14, 1814, when Francis Scott Key wrote the lyrics, I now understand the reason why "The Star Spangled

Banner was chosen to symbolize our nation. Let's take a closer look.

The Colonists were engaged in conflict with the British during the War Of 1812, and by 1814, each had prisoners of war. President James Madison decided to offer the British a chance to negotiate the release of the prisoners. Francis Scott Key, a lawyer from Baltimore, Maryland, was chosen to represent us. He was sent to a ship to discuss the trade with the British Admiral in charge. The British were holding about a thousand of our prisoners below deck on multiple ships. The Admiral, during negotiations, agreed to the exchange and Francis Scott Key went below deck to tell the prisoners they were being freed. However, the Admiral then came up with a disparaging statement, "We'll honor our commitment, but it won't matter. The war is over anyway. The men will be free but under British domination."

On that day, Francis Scott Key was given an ultimatum: "Lay down that American flag at Fort McHenry, which I see over there, or we're going to remove it from the face of the earth. The entire British war fleet of over 100 ships will shell that fort."

Key responded that it was not a military fort but filled with many women and children. The Admiral tried to convince Key that if they lowered the flag, he would stop the shelling. "We will know that they have surrendered, and you will be under British rule."

After refusing the Admiral's demands, Key was permitted to go below deck to talk to the prisoners. They asked him to tell them what was happening. Key related the scene to the prisoners. He then returned to the deck.

As the shelling continued, the flag could still be seen on the ramparts. The Admiral approached Key and said, "Your people are insane by not lowering that flag. Don't they understand that this is an impossible situation."

Key responded, "according to George Washington, an American will die on his feet before he lives on his knees."

The Admiral said, "Every cannon is focused on that flag and still it remains aloft."

For the next 3 hours, the artillery continued bombarding the fort mercilessly. Key could hear the men down below praying, "God keep that flag flying."

When the sun rose, through the smoke, there flew the flag, in shreds, but still flying. The flagpole was at a crazy angle but the flag held on.

When Key got to the fort and saw the carnage, he noted that men, women, and children had held that flag up until they died. Their bodies were then removed, and others took their place. Patriot's bodies held that flagpole up despite the terrible cost.

Finally, on December 24, the war ended with a treaty.

Francis Scott Key was a gifted poet. Inspired by the sight of the American flag flying over Fort McHenry the morning after the bombardment, he composed the first verse on the back of a letter. Once back in Baltimore, he completed four more verses and copied them onto a sheet of paper. Shortly after he finished, two Baltimore newspapers published his poem, and by mid-October, it appeared in at least seventeen other papers up and down the East coast.

Over the years, there were a number of controversies and conflicts that stopped the adoption of Key's poem to become our National Anthem. Despite these issues, a century after Key wrote it, the first stanza of the "Star Spangled Banner" was signed into law as our National Anthem by President Herbert Hoover on March 2, 1941.

When you examine the lyrics, you realize the true significance of Francis Scott Key's immortal words inspired by the conflict and the sacrifice of the defenders of our flag.

The Star-Spangled Banner

"O say can you see by the dawn's early light,

What so proudly we hail'd

at the twilight's last gleaming.

Whose broad stripes and bright stars

through the perilous fight

O'er the ramparts we watch'd

were so gallantly streaming?

And the rockets red glare,

the bombs bursting in air,

Gave proof through the night

that our flag was still there.

O say does that star-spangled banner yet wave

O'er the land of the free

and the home of the brave?

Key wrote more verses, but the others were not designated as part of our anthem, although sometimes we do hear the 4th verse sung. Here are the other verses:

Verse 2

On the shore dimly seen
through the mists of the deep
Where the foe's haughty host
in dread silence reposes,
What is that which the breeze,
o'er the towering steep,
As it fitfully blows,
half conceals, half discloses?
Now it catches the gleam
of the morning's first beam,
In full glory reflected now shines in the stream,
'Tis the star-spangled banner –
O long may it wave
O'er the land of the free
and the home of the brave!

Verse 3

And where is that band
who so vauntingly swore,
That the havoc of war
and the battle's confusion
A home and a country should leave us no more?
Their blood has wash'd out
their footstep's pollution.
No refuge could save
the hireling and slave
From the terror of flight
or the gloom of the grave,
And the star-spangled banner triumph doth wave
O'er the land of the free
and the home of the brave.

This last stanza might be familiar to you. It
is sometimes sung in addition to the official
Star-spangled Banner.

Verse 4

O thus be it ever

when freemen shall stand
Between their lov'd home
and the war's desolation!
Blessed with vict'ry and peace
may the heav'n rescued land
Praise the power that hath made
and preserv'd us a nation!
Then conquer we must,
when our cause it is just,
And this be our motto -
"In God is our trust,"
And the star-spangled banner
in triumph shall wave
O'er the land of the free
and the home of the brave.

The "Star Spangled Banner" declares we are united as a nation under our flag. We should sing it proudly as our anthem stating who we are as Americans, for all the world to hear and see.

EPILOGUE

We are united when we take pride in singing our National Anthem; when we cheer for our athletes at the International Olympics; and when we support our troops put in harm's way.

Irving Berlin, a Jewish immigrant wrote, "This is my country, land that I love." Like him, I'm proud to be an American. Throughout my life, I've been told that you have to accept the bad along with the good. I believe we can improve. I've also been told that "if you walk in someone else's shoes, you might see their problems are worse than yours." So, I try to see things from other's situations and points of view. I also always focus on the positive, even when things look dark.

America is a beautiful country with a wondrous and unique topography. It is a land that offers excellent opportunities. The dilemma is how we accept each individual and group and make it possible for them to take advantage of their connection with our great nation.

Self-examination and the courage to admit to bias and unhelpful behavior may be our greatest tools for change. Allowing ourselves to be vulnerable enough to recognize our ignorance and insecurities takes courage and love for our nation. I believe the most loving thing a person, or a group of people, can do is to examine the ways in which their own insecurities and assumptions interfere with others' abilities to thrive. Please join me and open your heart and mind to the possibility that you...yes, even well-intentioned you...have room to change and grow, so that we can all work with people of all colors and ethnicities to co-create communities that can unite, strengthen, and prosper.

Let's think about what we have in this country: the ability to be who we are without reprisal or condemnation, and how we should cherish the things that bring us together rather than those that tear us apart.

THAT IS THE PROMISE OF AMERICA AND WE CAN MAKE THAT PROMISE A REALITY IF WE UNITE.

ABOUT THE AUTHOR

S andy Solomon's first book, Snapshots, is a
memoir, which brought out the desire to be
a writer when she was a teenager.

Everyone has stories to tell about their lives,
but putting it in writing makes the memories and

highlights the experiences. At 16 years old, Sandy started a pen pal relationship with a complete stranger in the Marines, who was a friend of an acquaintance. That Marine became her husband and they were married for 63 years.

The Land Of Imperfection makes her audience realize that America is not united and the flaws are tearing us apart.

ALSO BY SANDY SOLOMON

Snapshots: Stories of My Life

What memories would you include as SNAPSHOTS of your life?

Sandy Solomon, a New York girl, had a life full of challenges and adventures that she wanted to share with her family and closest friends. As you read of her fascinating life, you will feel as if you are making a wonderful new friend, someone who cares.

Made in the USA
Columbia, SC
15 November 2023